OXFORD

WILD READS

Dinosaurs

Paul May

D1375023

OXFORD
UNIVERSITY PRESS

This book belongs to:

OXFORD
UNIVERSITY PRESS

Great Clarendon Street, Oxford OX2 6DP
Oxford University Press is a department of the University of Oxford.
It furthers the University's objective of excellence in research, scholarship,
and education by publishing worldwide in

Oxford   New York

Auckland   Cape Town   Dar es Salaam   Hong Kong   Karachi
Kuala Lumpur   Madrid   Melbourne   Mexico City   Nairobi
New Delhi   Shanghai   Taipei   Toronto

With offices in

Argentina   Austria   Brazil   Chile   Czech Republic   France   Greece
Guatemala   Hungary   Italy   Japan   Poland   Portugal   Singapore
South Korea   Switzerland   Thailand   Turkey   Ukraine   Vietnam

Oxford is a registered trade mark of Oxford University Press
in the UK and in certain other countries

Text © Paul May
Illustrations © Steve Kirk
The moral rights of the author have been asserted

Database right Oxford University Press (maker)

This edition 2009

British Library Cataloguing in Publication Data

Data available

ISBN: 978-0-19-911927-1

1 3 5 7 9 10 8 6 4 2

Printed in China
Paper used in the production of this book is a natural,
recyclable product made from wood grown in sustainable forests.
The manufacturing process conforms to the environmental
regulations of the country of origin.

Contents

▶ Real, live dinosaurs

Would you like to see a dinosaur? A real, live dinosaur? Well, maybe you can! Look out of the window. Birds are everywhere,

up in the sky, or pecking at the grass. A bird is a special kind of dinosaur – a dinosaur with feathers and wings!

A bird's skeleton looks like a dinosaur's skeleton. Look for yourself, and see.

bird skeleton

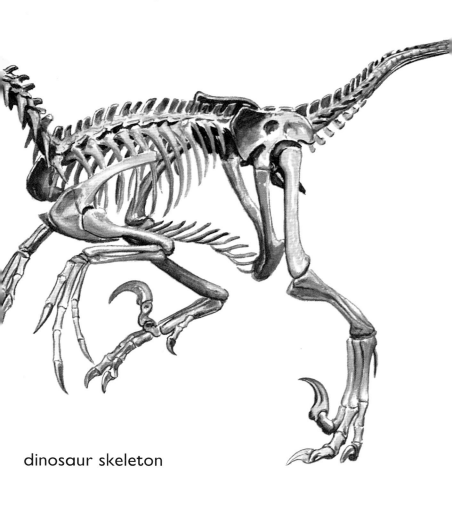

dinosaur skeleton

Watch how a bird walks. Watch how a bird pecks. Perhaps that is how a dinosaur moved. Birds can help us to imagine how the dinosaurs lived…

▶ 200 million years ago

It is hot. Insects buzz. Small animals scurry along the ground. Strange plants tower in the air. A frog hops by.

And then the earth begins to shake. The trees tremble, and giant footsteps crash through the forest.

A brachiosaurus is coming.

BOOM!

BOOM!

BOOM!

Did you know...
Dinosaurs lived on the earth for more than 170 **million** years. Human beings have only been here for about 200 **thousand** years – so far.

Brachiosaurus is bigger than a house. It munches leaves from the treetops. Its legs are like tree trunks, but it started out small. It grew from an egg, just like a bird!

brachiosaurus
(brak-ee-oh-**saw**-rus)

▶ Dinosaur babies

Life was dangerous for a dinosaur egg.
Lizards ate dinosaur eggs.
Small mammals ate dinosaur eggs.
Some dinosaurs ate dinosaur eggs!

Dinosaurs like orodromeus looked after their eggs. They built their nests close to other nests, and then they guarded them. They put leaves on top of their eggs to keep them warm.

When the babies hatched they could already walk. They walked around near their nest and picked up food – just like baby chickens. Their mums and dads looked after them until they were big enough to look after themselves.

orodromeus (**or**-oh-**drom**-ee-us)

maiasaura
(**my**-ah-**saw**-rah)

Dinosaurs like maiasaura looked after their babies too. When the babies were born they were weak and small, like baby blackbirds. Their mums and dads fed them until they were big enough to leave the nest.

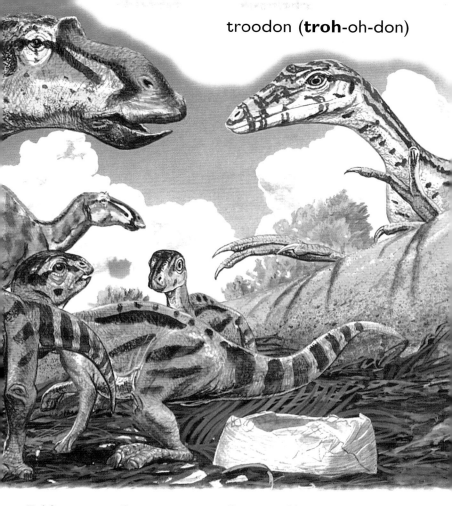

troodon (**troh**-oh-don)

Life was dangerous for a dinosaur baby. A dinosaur baby was easy to catch. A dinosaur baby had to learn fast about the dangers all around it. Each kind of dinosaur had its own special way of keeping safe.

▶ Keeping safe

Diplodocus kept safe by being big. They could squash their enemies with their enormous feet, or knock them down with their enormous tails.

Hypsilophodon kept safe by being small and quick. Hypsilophodon probably moved in herds and ate small plants. If they spotted danger they could stand up on their long hind legs, and race away from trouble.

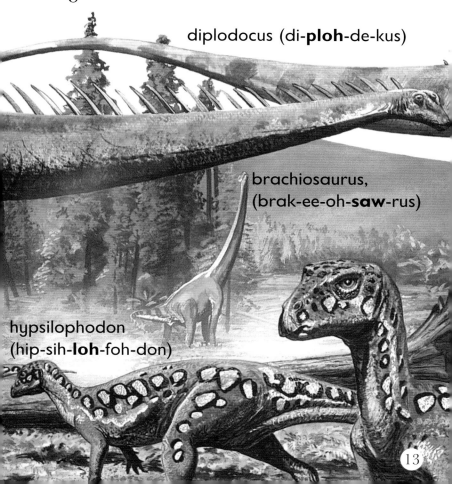

diplodocus (di-**ploh**-de-kus)

brachiosaurus, (brak-ee-oh-**saw**-rus)

hypsilophodon (hip-sih-**loh**-foh-don)

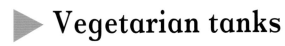

Vegetarian tanks

These dinosaurs were armour-plated, like tanks. They couldn't run very fast, but that didn't matter. They were hard to kill because their bodies were covered with scales and spikes.

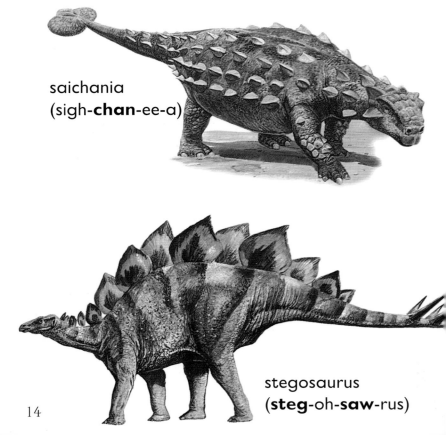

saichania
(sigh-**chan**-ee-a)

stegosaurus
(**steg**-oh-**saw**-rus)

edmontonia
(ed-mon-**tone**-ee-a)

If another dinosaur attacked them they could fight back. Some fought with huge claws. Some fought with tails like clubs. Some had horns and some had strangely-shaped heads.

But these dinosaurs didn't **eat** other dinosaurs. They only ate plants. They shredded them up with their strange teeth.

▶ Meat-eaters

Some dinosaurs had terrible teeth and terrible claws, like lions and tigers today. They ate meat – every kind of meat. Insects, frogs, lizards, mammals – and other dinosaurs!

Some meat-eaters were not much bigger than your cat. They ate lizards and insects, and small mammals.

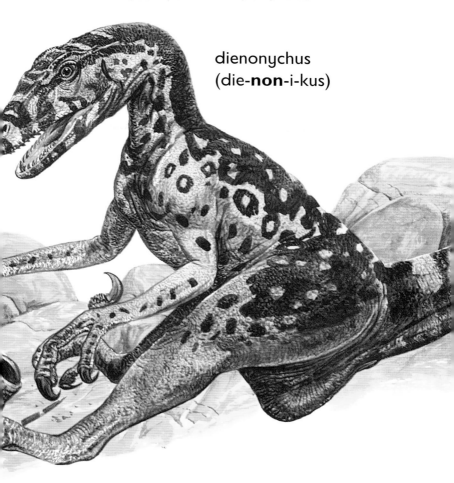

dienonychus
(die-**non**-i-kus)

Some were a little bigger. They
hunted in packs, like wolves. They
could surround a bigger dinosaur
and kill it.

And then there were the biggest
meat-eaters of all...

**tyrannosaurus rex
(tie-ran-oh-saw-rus)**

Tyrannosaurus rex was as big as a truck. It had a huge head, and its teeth were like knives. It rammed into other dinosaurs, and its teeth sliced their flesh.

Maybe it ate dead animals too. Maybe tyrannosaurus **stole** its meals from other meat-eaters. You didn't argue with tyrannosaurus rex!

▶ Amazing dinosaur legs

The dinosaurs ruled the earth for millions of years. But why?

Well, maybe it was because of their legs!

Try walking like a lizard. It's hard work. Your tummy drags along the ground. Your arms ache, and it's very slow.

Now try walking like a dinosaur. Much better! And much stronger too.

Brachiosaurus's legs were huge and strong, like pillars under a bridge. Only tucked-under legs could hold up the weight of brachiosaurus.

Hypsilophodon's legs were delicate, like the legs of a gazelle. Only tucked-under legs could help hypsilophodon to race away from trouble.

Dinosaur bones

a dinosaur dying

Sometimes, when a dinosaur died, its bones sank into soft mud at the bottom of a lake. Sometimes, dry desert sand covered the bones.

Very slowly, the dinosaur bones turned to rock. They became fossil bones.

Millions of years went by. Then people walked on the earth. People found the bones.

"Perhaps they are the bones of dragons!" said people in China.

"Perhaps they are the bones of giants," other people said.

Did you know...
The word dinosaur comes from Greek and means "terrible lizard".

And then someone worked out the truth.

"These are the bones of animals," they said. "But these animals must have been huge. There are no animals like this on the earth today. They are like enormous lizards. We will call them **dinosaurs**."

dinosaur footprints

Dinosaur detectives

All over the world people began to search for dinosaur bones. Scientists are still searching today. They have found dinosaur skeletons, dinosaur footprints and dinosaur eggs.

Finding out about dinosaurs is like being a detective. Scientists look at the fossils and try to imagine – how did these bones fit together? What were the dinosaurs really like?

Sometimes the scientists make mistakes. Sometimes they argue! But all the time they learn new things. There is still plenty of work for dinosaur detectives to do!

▶ The end of the dinosaurs?

For millions of years there were dinosaurs. Then a terrible disaster happened. The earth grew cold and dark. But why?

iguanodon
(ig-**wha**-noh-don)

Scientists think that a meteorite smashed into the earth. Maybe volcanoes erupted too. Dust and smoke hid the warm sun, and the dinosaurs died.

albertosaurus
(al-**bert**-oh-**saw**-rus)

But other creatures lived on. They lived on in the cold, dark world. Mammals lived on. Frogs, crocodiles, insects and fish lived on. And one special kind of dinosaur lived on.

65 MYA

So look out of your window and watch some real, live dinosaurs.

The birds.

Glossary

 fossil Fossils are the remains of plants and animals that have become hard and rock-like while they have been under the ground.   **22, 25**

 mammal A mammal has warm blood, a backbone and (usually) hair. Mammal mothers feed their babies with milk from their breasts.   **8, 16, 28**

 meteorite When a lump of rock or metal from outer space crashes into the earth, it is called a meteorite.   **27**

scientist Scientists are people who study the world. The scientists who study the fossils of dinosaurs are called palaeontologists (pal-ee-on-tol-o-jists). **25**

 skeleton A skeleton is the framework of bones inside the body of an animal. **5**

 volcano Melted rock, gas and ash are forced out from the inside of the earth through volcanoes. **27**

MYA MYA stands for millions of years ago.

OXFORD

WILD READS

WILD READS will help your child develop a love of reading and a lasting curiosity about our world. See the websites and places to visit below to learn more about dinosaurs.

Dinosaurs

WEBSITES
Fun and Games
http://www.nhm.ac.uk/kids-only/fun-games/index.html

http://www.kidsdinos.com/

PLACES TO VISIT
The Dinosaur Museum
http://www.thedinosaurmuseum.com/
The award-winning and only museum on mainland Britain dedicated to dinosaurs.

The Natural History Museum
http://www.nhm.ac.uk/

OR HAVE A TRULY MONSTER DAY OUT AT THESE ADVENTURE PARKS
The Big Dinosaur Adventure
http://www.dinosauradventure.co.uk/

The Dinosaur Park
http://www.thedinosaurpark.co.uk/